UN-DECEIVED

FOUR YEARS,
CHAINED TO THE TRUTH,
FACE OF DECEPTION

A Trilogy by Mary Webb Kirkpatrick

WESTBOW
PRESS®
A DIVISION OF THOMAS NELSON
& ZONDERVAN

WestBow Press books may be ordered through booksellers or by contacting:

WestBow Press
A Division of Thomas Nelson & Zondervan
1663 Liberty Drive
Bloomington, IN 47403
www.westbowpress.com
844-714-3454

Holy Bible, New Living Translation, copyright © 1996, 2004, 2015 by
Tyndale House Foundation. Used by permission of Tyndale House
Publishers, Inc., Carol Stream, Illinois 60188. All rights reserved.

ISBN: 978-1-9736-6588-5 (sc)
ISBN: 978-1-9736-6589-2 (e)

Print information available on the last page.

WestBow Press rev. date: 05/05/2023

CONTENTS

Mary's story is the story of her finding the narrow way and her courageous pursuit to walk down the path that so few find. It reminds me of Song of Songs 1:8, "Listen, my radiant one—if you ever lose sight of me, just follow in my footsteps where I lead my lovers. Come with your burdens and cares. Come to the place near the sanctuary of my shepherds." Through Mary, Jesus is saying, "Come and follow Me." Follow Mary's lead and you will find Him. Take His hand, and you will find True Life.

Kathryn Lindsey Kiser,
author of Piercing the Night

To know Mary is to love Mary. Readers of this book are in for a treat as she shares her journey back to God through His Word. I think her story will inspire you to open up His Word and reconnect with the Lover of your soul.

Stephanie Shaw,
friend and Licensed Therapist

PART I
FOUR YEARS

CHAPTER I

DECEMBER 19, 2014

My turning point came December 19, 2014, the first day of my Christmas break as a teacher. That was the day I came to the end of myself. I was sick and tired of my life spinning out of control. Most days I felt absent. I was there, but not all of me. I was really eager to get out of the caged prison I had been trapped in for so many years. I was out of control and searching for something to fill the emptiness.

I was exhausted. I remember having conversations with God and asking God to please come and get me if things didn't change soon. On many occasions I felt like Hannah in the Old Testament. Her prayer for a child was so desperate that she would open her mouth to pray but not a sound was uttered. Her mouth was moving but nothing came out. My prayers had become just like that. I was so lost. I had wandered so far off the path. I finally looked up to Heaven and said, "Father, how do I get back to you? What do I need to do to see Your face again? How do I hear Your voice again? I miss You Papa." So, the Father and I began having conversations. This was the beginning of my search.

"You want to know how to see my face again?" Father asked. "You want to know how to get back to me? You want to hear my voice again? Read the letter I sent you." I was silent for a moment, and then I began to argue and reason with Father whether or not I would do what He asked me to do. "God, I am not reading this

3

Bible in the King James Version from cover to cover," I said. Now notice that this is not at all what He said; it was what I heard. I continued to argue with the Father, telling him what I was not going to do, until there was silence again. Finally, I asked, "Father, can I read this letter in another translation?" A moment went by, and Father said, "Okay." So I did what all good procrastinators do: I asked one last question. "Can I read the letter from The Message Bible translation?" I asked. He quickly responded, "Yes, you may."

Even with this conversation it still took me some time to get my mind on board with this quest. I was wondering what the urgency was all about until the day the Father said something that got my attention. "Mary, until you finish reading, I cannot move you to your next level," He said. "In fact, I can do nothing until you're done reading. I need you to know Me. I don't want you to just know about Me. I don't want you to just know your pastor's God or your daughters' God or the God you hear preachers talk about on Youtube. I want you to experience Me and get to know Me for yourself."

I began my quest. I made the decision to turn my back on everything and everyone that had kept me from pursuing God the previous four years. I disappeared from sight. I turned off my cell phone, logged out of my computer, and put Facebook on hold. I even stopped listening to worship music. Instead, I opened up the letter and began reading, "First this: God created the Heavens and the Earth" (Genesis 1:1, The Message).

The Word began to do what no one else was able to do for years: it began to soften a heart that was hard as stone. I found myself becoming less and less angry. I began to realize my anger stemmed from believing too many lies. I was no longer consumed by my hurts and wounds because my focus was being redirected. The darkness didn't seem so dark anymore. The light began to shine brighter and brighter.

I no longer felt hopeless, like there was no way out of the prison

I had built for myself. I no longer had a "what's the use?" attitude. Suicidal thoughts began to diminish. Faith began to emerge back to the surface. I could envision hope. I even began to think of ways of escape from the place I was in. Ultimately, as I began to take hold of truth, God gave me the ability to find the way out. It was not in my own strength but in the strength and the life of the written Word of God.

I dealt with depression for quite some time, even after I began to read. For the next two months, I did not sleep or eat much. Prior to this appetite loss, I had already lost a total of seventy pounds the unintelligent way: stress, unhealthy lifestyle, and poor diet. During these two months of download, the Word became my source, the only thing I needed or wanted. The more I read, the more I wanted to read.

Father had told me that until I read His letter, He couldn't move me. I wanted to know what that new season was that God had in store for me. I was on a mission. My daily goal was to get into my bed soon after work, turn on my Kindle and read. As I would read, I'd fall asleep. Often, I would wake up in the middle of the night and continue reading until I fell back asleep. If I woke up again, I would read again until I fell asleep. During the day, I began to crave God and His Word uncontrollably. In my classroom, my students had silent reading every day after lunch. I began to use this time to read. As the children read silently, so did I. This went on for two months. Yes, I said two months. That's how long it took me to read the letter.

Even before I finished all of His letter, God began revealing things to me. After reading just half of His letter, Father showed me three traits about Himself. First, He loves His people, He loves me, and He treasures His family. He doesn't like when his family is treated wrongly. Multiple times Father declared He would bless those who blessed Israel, but He also declared He would curse those who cursed Israel. God loves His family.

Second, when God became angry with His family, He would

always show mercy and love. In the Old Testament when Pharaoh asked Moses to pray, Moses would pray and God's heart would begin to show compassion. In Romans 2:14, the Bible tells us it is the goodness of God that leads a man to repentance. Third, Father showed me that He always provides a way out of any circumstance. God will make a way where there seems to be no way.

When I read the second half of the letter (New Testament) these three traits of God settled in my spirit. Because these three traits are woven into the fabric of God, I knew they should be woven into the fabric of me. I should love as God loves. I should show mercy because of the mercy shown to me. I should never give up on people no matter what it may look like. I'm so glad He didn't give up on me.

I think God is concerned about the process but I think He is more eager to see the finished work. He did say, "To him who overcomes I will grant to sit with Me on my throne, as I also overcame and sat down with My Father on His throne" (Revelation 3:21, NKJV). My feat was complete: I read the letter. Now that I knew my God a little better, the real work could begin.

CHAPTER II

GOD DOESN'T TEMPT US
JAMES 1:13-15

M ost would applaud my incredible feat of reading the Bible all the way through, because most believers never do. Some would rejoice and thank God that a sheep that once was lost now is found and brought back into the fold. I have realized one thing: this was not the end but the beginning of the road back to God. The battle of my mind was won but the war was far from over.

I'm aware it's already won as His Word proclaims. In Colossians 2:13-15 (NIV), the Bible says "When you were dead in your sins and in the uncircumcision of your flesh, God made you alive with Christ. He forgave us all our sins, having canceled the charge of our legal indebtedness, which stood against us and condemned us; he has taken it away, nailing it to the cross. And having disarmed the powers and authorities, he made a public spectacle of them, triumphing over them by the cross." We need to remember the law of sowing and reaping. Sowing and reaping is still a principle that works in the earth much like gravity is a principle. What goes up must come down. In contrast the things we sow will produce fruit, either good and bad.

During this revival of my spirit, my flesh was still reaping the seeds of death that were planted long before December 19, 2014. Remember it was my spirit that was renewed; my flesh was (and still is) at war with the spirit. I'm still waiting for my flesh to catch up to the Word that has been poured into me. It's kind of like this: just because you decide to begin eating right and exercising, it doesn't mean your body is going to automatically become your dream body. It's going to take a process of new habits and new mindsets. The same goes for the flesh. There needs to be new habits, new mindsets, and new seed in order to get a different kind of result.

James 1:13-15 reveals that I was drawn away by my own lust, and, when I was enticed, conception took place (the seed was given life). As I gave the seed of my own lust permission to mature, sin was born. Full-grown sin results in death. This will be the result *every single time*.

I do not believe you can be drawn away by something you have no desire for. I also believe that what you desire is the very thing that will cause you to be drawn away or drawn to Him. So, I had to either change my desires by changing what and who I let influence me, or do nothing and continue to be drawn away by those desires and stay the same.

Like most I was drawn away by something I already had an appetite for. I allowed the seed (the thought) to propel me to the next level. If you keep thinking on something long enough, it will come to pass whether good or bad. It works both ways. It's like this: what you feed your physical body affects how your physical body functions and to what capacity. It's no different in regards to your spirit man. If you feed on murmuring and complaining, it will affect what blessings come your way.

Remember, it was the children (the next generation) of the original Israelites who came out of the desert and went into the promised land. Scripture states, "Nevertheless, as surely as I live and as surely as the glory of the Lord fills the whole earth, not one of those who saw my glory and the signs I performed in Egypt and in the wilderness but who disobeyed me and tested me ten times—not one of them will ever see the land I promised on oath to their ancestors. No one who has treated me with contempt will ever see it. But because my servant Caleb has a different spirit and follows me wholeheartedly, I will bring him into the land he went to, and his descendants will inherit it" (Numbers 14:21-24, NIV).

The process goes on. When I've been enticed, that seed has grown into desire, and that desire has my attention. As time goes on, it is now requiring more from me. This object of desire is luring me away by making me excited about the idea that giving into this desire is what I want and need to be fulfilled.

All this process was happening in regards to my flesh. My spirit couldn't help me then. It couldn't even put up a fight. First, it was asleep and needed to be awakened. Second, my spirit had no weapons to fight with because I hadn't equipped it. The Word was the weapon I needed to fight and win this battle but at the time I was unable to make that connection. It really wasn't even a matter of fighting the battle. I just had to read the Word, declare the Word, and the Word would do what it was meant to do.

This process happened because I gave this desire my full attention and left it unaddressed for too long. The desire was given the opportunity to grow and become full-grown sin. It was like the wheels were set in motion and there was nothing I could do to stop it. Sin was on its way.

Romans 7:14- 25 (NIV) describes this season of my life. I felt like I was trapped inside a vacuum where there was no way out. I wanted to break out but felt helpless to do so. I wanted to do the right thing but always found myself doing the wrong thing. I literally felt the weight of the chains of sin in the spirit. I felt such heaviness and unrest. I could not provide a way out of my own bondage. I was in a hopeless situation, and that's why the thoughts of suicide intensified. I figured if this was the way I was going to live surely dying would be better.

Some of us are a little slower in figuring out obvious things. For years, I struggled and fought a battle I was never really going to win because I was using the wrong weapons to fight with. I was fighting a spiritual battle with natural weapons. The Bible says in

Ephesians 6:12, "For our struggle is not against flesh and blood, but against the rulers, against the authorities, against the powers of this dark world and against the spiritual forces of evil in the heavenly realms" (NIV).

I found that when I stopped trying to *do* (or not to do in this case) and concentrated more on *being,* freedom became easy. I simply changed my focus. As I began to think on different things, the battle ground changed. Instead of fighting against the desires of my own lusts, I began to fight the good fight of faith. What is the good fight of faith you may ask? For me it was taking hold of eternal things that last forever and turning my back on earthly things that never fully satisfy anyway.

CHAPTER III

FOCUS
PHILIPPIANS 4:8

Weeks later, I was out for my daily walk through the neighborhood. Usually, I look straight ahead and focus on my next step. It's like I'm on an exercise mission, and I usually listen to either music or the Word for the hour-long walk. On this particular day, it was like I went into a trance for a few seconds. I was focused more on what was around me. I started looking at the tall grass I was walking by when all sorts of thoughts flooded my mind. I began to wonder what kind of animals were in that tall grass. I wondered when one would come popping out. I wondered how fast I could run to get away from it. Crazy, right? But real. I also noticed that when I put my eyes back on the path in front of me, those crazy thoughts went away almost as fast as they came flooding in.

I was reminded about a similar account in the Word when Peter walked on water in Matthew 14:28-29. As long as Peter kept his eyes on the One who walked on the water, he was able to walk on water too. The moment Peter began to look around at the waves and the storm, he began to sink, because His imagination was seeing something different. As soon as he called out for the Lord (put his focus back where it should have been), he was saved and back on top of the waves.

The Holy Spirit began to speak to me about *focus*. First, I

11

noticed that when I kept my head up and looked forward, I could see where I was going. I could see the next step. There was no guessing or wondering where to put my foot down next.

Second, the Holy Spirit told me if I keep my head up and focus on what's in front of me, I could see things coming. Nothing in front of me could take me by surprise. I didn't need to be concerned about what was behind me. The Word says I have goodness and mercy that follow me all the days of my life and that I will dwell in the house of the Lord forever (Psalm 23:6). The Word also tells me that He is my rear guard (Isaiah 52:12).

Third, the Holy Spirit was warning me to keep my eyes on the path and to always look ahead on that path. Paul tells us to press on to reach the end of the race and receive the heavenly prize for which God, through Christ Jesus, is calling us (Philippians 3:14, NIV). Proverbs 4:26 (AMP) instructs us to "Consider well *and* watch carefully the path of your feet, And all your ways will be steadfast *and* sure." It's important to keep your head up as you travel so that you can adjust your step as you need to; the alternative is stumbling. Also, when your head is up, you get a wider view—the whole picture.

The Bible says in I Corinthians 15:46 that the natural comes before the spiritual. Now let's shift from my walk (an example of the natural) into a spiritual application. Because I'm a teacher, I looked up the word *focus* and learned that it means to concentrate or to direct one's attention and efforts (Dictionary.com). The scripture in James 1:8 says that a double-minded man is "unstable in all his ways." Unstable means liable to fall or sway; wavering; and marked by emotional instability (Dictionary.com). Scripture goes on to say in verse 7, don't let this man think he should receive anything from the Lord.

On December 19, 2014, my spirit was renewed. My spirit man woke up, and my spirit man came alive. However, my mind, will, and emotions were still trapped in the old mindset. Awakening someone out of their spiritual slumber is the easy part. It's still a miracle, but getting the mind, will and emotions lined up with the renewed spirit is not easy. The war against spirit and flesh is no joke. The mind battle is the toughest battle you will ever fight. Whatever gets your mind has your attention. It steals your focus. My mind had been unstable for many years. I didn't know how to focus. I didn't know what it meant to think with a single mind. My thoughts were all over the map and changed with every circumstance. There was no constant, and no truth.

I believe this is why God required me to start this journey back to Him with the reading of his Word. In Judges 21:25, we are told that Israel didn't have a king so every man did what was right in his own eyes. I didn't have the King of kings reigning in my life, so I did what was right in my own eyes. That's why the Bible says in Proverb 14:12 there is a way that seems right to a man, but, in the end, it leads to death. I imagine God knew I had tried it my way long enough (for about five years), and He knew, in His infinite wisdom, that if I truly wanted to be free once and for all, I had to do it His way. If I was going to change, my thoughts had to change. My thoughts had to change and conform to God's thoughts. Romans 12:2 (NIV) says "Do not conform to the pattern of this world, but be transformed by the renewing of your mind. Then you will be able to test and approve what God's will is—his good, pleasing and perfect will."

Father wanted me to read the scripture from cover to cover. This was significant for me because in the past I had read it in bits and pieces—a scripture here and a scripture there and never in context. I would just find scripture for whatever I needed at the time and read that portion. Never once did I read it from cover to cover. This mandate from God put a whole new perspective on the Word for me. I began to see how things were tied together. For example, learning about the different genealogies was super fun. One that really blew my mind was Rahab the prostitute. If she had not come into the picture to save the spies sent by Joshua in the battle of Jericho, then she would have been destroyed like the rest of the people there in that city (Joshua 2). If she had been killed, then Boaz may have never been born because this was his mother. Even more, Jesus was to come from this line. This blew my mind! Reading the Word in sequence was literally like laying the foundation for my Christian faith. Every Christian should do it at least once. It's like I was learning about my heritage, and, because I understood my past, my future would look very different.

Another awesome result of reading the Word of God from cover to cover was truly understanding the New Testament. In the New Testament, many references are made to the Old Testament. Because I had read both, the New Testament now made a lot of sense. He truly was the same God in the New Testament that He was in the Old. Hebrews 13:8 (NIV) says, "Jesus Christ is the same yesterday and today and forever."

CHAPTER IV

MIND EXCHANGE

I had wandered so far away from God that walking with God felt foreign and uncomfortable. I didn't know the difference between what was fact and what was truth. I was living life according to my own interpretation of truth, and the way I reasoned and concluded life should be lived was contrary to the truth of God's Word. I made my own decisions based on how I felt, and I did what others did in order to fit in. Even more than that, I knew the amount of effort and energy it would take to live differently from the way I had become accustomed to living. I was just not motivated to make those changes at this stage of my life.

The realization that I had gotten this far off the path of life so impacted me that it sobered me. It scared me to think that my darkness had become light to me. The Bible warns in Matthew 6:23 (NIV), "If then the light within you is darkness, how great is that darkness!" My darkness had become very great! In fact, I was on the path of destruction.

It was time to take on the countless enemies of my mind that had set up and built fortified strongholds in strategic areas of my thinking. Trying to do this on my own without the aid of God's Word would have resulted in a sure defeat, every single time.

For the next year, my favorite word became, "No!" Every time a thought contrary to what I was reading in the Bible came up, I would immediately utter the word "No!" I could be driving down the road in my car, and a wrong thought would come across the window of my mind. With authority in my voice, I would say "No!" Then the thought would leave me as quick as it came, until the next opportunity. At the beginning stages of my renewing-the-mind journey, these opportunities would happen every hour on the hour.

The thoughts that took the longest to wash out were the thoughts that were triggered by memories from the previous five years. I would see a post on Facebook, hear someone's voice, pass by a favorite restaurant, or even hear a familiar song and be triggered. I finally had to shut it all off. I had to close my mind to anything and everything that looked or smelled like the world. For about one year, I spent a lot of time listening to sermons on Youtube. I only listened to worship music. My only reading consisted of the Word of God. I prayed in the Spirit most of my waking days during that first year. If it didn't look like or smell like Jesus, I didn't want any part of it. Ephesians 5: 25-27 (KJV) says, "Husbands, love your wives, even as Christ also loved the church, and gave himself for it; That he might sanctify and cleanse it with the washing of water by the word, That he might present it to himself a glorious church, not having spot, or wrinkle, or any such thing; but that it should be holy and without blemish." This is without a doubt a very accurate and life-saving scripture for me. During this first year, I lived my life very guarded, almost to the point of having a religious-spirit mindset. I was relentless in my journey for a renewed mind.

The washing of the Word is what began to transform my thinking, which transformed my heart, which in turn transformed my words, and, ultimately, transformed my life. I wish I could tell you this was the end of the renewing of my mind. Rather, this was the beginning stage of renewal, and it would be crucial to my survival during the next year. If my journey had not begun with the Word of God, I would not have made it through the unbearable battles in the days and years to come.

In order to become kingdom minded, I had to learn to take the words off the pages and aggressively assert them into the atmosphere of this fallen world. In many instances, I had to speak those things I wanted to see happen into existence. Romans 4:17 (KJV) says, "(As it is written, I have made thee a father of many nations,) before him whom he believed, even God, who quickeneth the dead, and calleth those things which be not as though they were."

During this second year, I had to keep reminding myself that my flesh is crazy and there is no good thing in this flesh. Romans 7:18 (KJV) says, "For I know that in me (that is, in my flesh,) dwelleth no good thing: for to will is present with me; but how to perform that which is good I find not." While "no" was still my favorite word, I was noticing I didn't have to say it as often. As I became convinced in my mind of a certain truth, I could no longer be attacked in that area. The continual washing of the Word was setting up its own strongholds in my mind to replace the former ones.

I didn't see this at first, but every time I screamed no, I was really resisting the devil. Every time I said no, the enemy had no other choice but to run. In James 4:7, I was told if I resist the devil, he will flee.

I had to exchange the object of my submission from my flesh to my spirit. Before I was submitting to the flesh and resisting the Spirit of God. Now I chose to submit to God and resist the devil. This was not a hard thing to do. As I submitted my mind and my thoughts to the Word of God, my contrary thoughts began to go away.

Eventually my thoughts became more like His thoughts. I found myself spending less time trying to change my mind and more time just resting and enjoying my new found peace of my mind. I was becoming more like the renewed spirit in me and less like the unrenewed flesh that constantly fought against God.

CHAPTER V

DON'T LET A DAY GO BY

One day Father God showed me an open vision. I guess that's what you call it. I was wide awake, and it was like time was suspended for a few moments. I believe it was God's response to a question I had asked in the previous year. I asked Him about Matthew 7:13-14 (NLT) which says, "You can enter God's Kingdom only through the narrow gate. The highway to hell is broad, and its gate is wide for the many who choose that way. But the gateway to life is very narrow and the road is difficult, and only a few ever find it."

I saw myself looking at a piece of cardboard paper that had a multitude of black dots on it. It was kind of like the dots you see in a cellular phone ad when they talk about the phone coverage of any particular company. It was all a big blur to me at first. In the vision, I had a hand-held magnifying glass, and, as I began looking through it, I started to see more detail. The little dots began taking a different shape. They looked like little heads with long and short hair. Then I began to see bodies appearing on these suspended heads. They looked as though they were marching in unison but with no sense of urgency or emotion. There were thousands of rows of people marching. As the magnifying glass brought this scene into clearer focus, I saw another line of people that was marching down the middle of the other marching brigade. This was a single file line of people, one right behind the other. This line seemed to march a little quicker than the others and with a purpose, like they knew their destination.

In my finite thinking, I imagined the phrase "narrow is the gate" to mean that a hundred people could fit through the gate at one time. This seemed reasonable to me because there are almost 8 billion people on planet earth. However, the next thing that the Father showed me was so sobering I began to fear and tremble. Father showed me that the line that marched with purpose wasn't a hundred people across, or ten people across, or even two people across. Father showed me this narrow gate was a single-file line. Then He uttered these words, He said, "My people don't even have a clue what that narrow road looks like." This was a very sobering picture of events, but it made a lot of sense in light of 2 Corinthians 5:10 (NLT) that says, "For we must all stand before Christ to be judged. We will each receive whatever we deserve for the good or evil we have done in this earthly body."

Father also showed me another vision of a highway. He showed me walking down this highway while He urged me to stay inside the boundaries of the yellow and white lines. After a while, He showed me this same highway suspended in mid-air. He showed me that one wrong step over either line could cause harm, or maybe even death, if you're not careful to stay where it's safe (inside your lines).

The Father was letting me know that one day out of His Word could be a matter of life and death. I began to think about the people who only read their Word when the pastor reads it on Sunday morning. I began to think, where are they? Have they already gone over the side of the road? Are they even on the road? And what about me? Why would I ever take one step without hearing what the Word tells me to do next?

There is so much goodness available in reading the Word daily. For example, there is mercy available to me each day. The Bible says in Lamentations 3:22-23 (KJV), "It is of the LORD'S mercies that we are not consumed, because his compassions fail not. They are new every morning: great is thy faithfulness." Psalm 103:2 (ESV) tells me to "Bless the LORD, O my soul, and forget not all his benefits." To miss a day would be to miss my portion of mercy that is new every morning.

Identity is found in the Bible. Psalm 139:14 (NIV) says "I am fearfully and wonderfully made." That means I am beautiful, amazing, astonishing and a wonder. According to Genesis 1:27, I was made in His image.

Healing is found in the Bible. At one point my heart was hard as a rock. You know how hard play dough gets if you leave it uncovered or don't tend to it by putting it away in the sealed container to protect it? If you've ever made the mistake of leaving it out so it hardened, then you know you have to put a little water on it to soften it up to make it pliable again. It's similar to a potter with a ball of clay. The potter constantly uses water as he molds the clay into an image. The Word is water for your soul. A geologist will tell you if water runs over rock long enough, it will make the rough edges smooth. Water can even change the shape of a rock. In this instance on my journey this is what the Word did to my heart.

Hebrews 4:12 (NLT) reads, "For the word of God is alive and powerful. It is sharper than the sharpest two-edged sword, cutting between soul and spirit, between joint and marrow. It exposes our innermost thoughts and desires." The Word of God did what no person on earth could have done. The Word performed surgery on my heart; it broke it all apart, and then put it back together again.

Correction and preparation are found in the Bible. In 2 Timothy 3:16-17 (NLT), it says that, "All Scripture is inspired by God and is useful to teach us what is true and to make us realize what is wrong in our lives. It corrects us when we are wrong and teaches us to do what is right. God uses it to prepare and equip his people to do every good work." I am still a long way away from perfect. The Word is continuing to heal me on a daily basis.

Jeremiah 17:14 (NLT) says, "O Lord, if you heal me, I will be truly healed; if you save me, I will be truly saved. My praises are for you alone!" The Father's Word has truly done a work in me and is continuing to heal me.

However, the most important reason I can never let a day go by without reading this Letter is because it reveals who my Father is. This was why He urged me to begin my journey back to Him by reading the Letter.

His Letter has the answer for every question in life—every one of them. This Letter is your map for life. If you don't read the map, you won't be able to get to where you need to go because you won't know how to get there. On my journey, I realized that the answer to every question is Jesus. For these reasons I will never let a day go by that I don't feed on His Word.

CHAPTER VI

AFTER THE WORD

After I read the Letter through once, I began reading it a second time. The Bible is a book you could read a million times and get something new every single time. One time, I read the same chapter three days in a row. I color coded my notes, and the notes were different all three days. This to me is a perfect example of the "new mercies every morning" that the prophet Jeremiah spoke about in Lamentations.

The Word is amazing and full of life. The Word is a lamp unto my feet (Psalm 119:105), sharper than any two-edged sword (Hebrews 4:12) and powerful enough to soften the hardest heart; but something else was needed. I needed a "next level" something. I needed a power punch to put the devil back in his place which is under my feet (Ephesians 1:22).

I believe that during this season of my life the Word was the most effective weapon I could have had. I believe it's the most powerful weapon because when you have the Word you have Jesus Himself. In John 1:1 (NIV), it reads "In the beginning was the Word, and the Word was with God, and the Word was God." Later in John 1:14, it reads, "The Word became flesh and made his dwelling among us." The Word is legit.

In Acts 6:4 (NKJV), it says that the disciples desired to give themselves over continually "to prayer and to the ministry of the word." In Ephesians 6:17-18, it says "take the helmet of salvation, and the sword of the Spirit, which is the word of God; praying always with all prayer and supplication in the Spirit." These were but a few scriptures that reminded me that, along with the Word, I also needed to develop an effective prayer life. I came to understand that prayer is simply talking to the Father. Father God is very interested in relationships. Now that I had read about Him in the amazing Letter He left for me, it was time to get to know Him on a more personal level.

I began talking to the Father daily. I asked Him about everything. I wanted to be able to recognize His voice for myself. I would ask Him simple things. For example, one time I was going to an interview and put on regular business attire with a blazer. I didn't feel comfortable in what I was wearing for reasons unknown to me. So, I simply asked the Father what He wanted me to wear to this interview. He asked me, "What would make you feel more comfortable?" So, I went to my closet and changed into something casual. I went to the interview feeling very comfortable and more confident, and it was an amazing interview which ultimately landed me the job. I learned that day that Father cares about things that concern me—even what to wear on an interview. These kinds of conversations went on for months. I really got to know His heart and His goodness towards me.

Yet, even though my prayer life had gone to a whole new level in my relationship with the Father, there were still times that I was plagued by wrong thoughts. I was still being harassed by my past. I was still experiencing feelings of betrayal and feelings that I didn't matter in the big scheme of things.

I knew there was more. Now that I had read the Letter and was talking to the Father on a more personal level, I began to trust Him more. I began hearing His voice without even having to ask a question. In Matthew 6:8 (NLT), it says, "your Father knows exactly what you need even before you ask him!" I was experiencing this verse in my life.

In Isaiah 55:11(AMP) I came across an amazing set of words that transformed my prayer life even more. It says, "So will My word be which goes out of My mouth; It will not return to Me void (useless, without result), Without accomplishing what I desire, And without succeeding in the matter for which I sent it." As I meditated on this verse, I realized this was the key I needed to open the next door of freedom in my life. I had to take the words off the pages and begin speaking them in the atmosphere. This was good news because I knew whenever I spoke His Word into the atmosphere it would not come back without accomplishing what it was sent out to do.

One day, my roommate had a prayer request for a friend's son. Her son and a friend had gone out hiking and 48 hours later they had not yet returned home. While these boys were seasoned hikers, an unexpected storm system had come over the mountains right where they went hiking, and they were lost. The search and rescue team was unable to search for them until the following morning because of the storm. Rather than wait, we began to pray the words from the Bible. We prayed Jeremiah 29:11 (AMP), where the Father says "For I know the plans *and* thoughts that I have for you,' says the Lord, 'plans for peace and well-being and not for disaster, to give you a future and a hope." We prayed to dispatch angels, like Psalm 103:20 (AMP), which says, "Bless the LORD, you His angels, You mighty ones who do His commandments, Obeying the voice of His word!". Within hours we got word these boys were found alive and well.

With this new knowledge of how to use the Word of God as a real weapon in prayer, I began to apply this to the battles that were raging inside of me (e.g. wrong thinking, holding on to offenses). As I began to speak words from this Letter out of my mouth, these words came off the page and began to accomplish what they set out to do in me. My life was forever changed. No longer was I fighting the battles, but the Word was fighting for me. In 2 Chronicles 20:15 (AMP), it says "The LORD says this to you: 'Be not afraid or dismayed at this great multitude, for the battle is not yours, but God's."

CHAPTER VII

PRAYER THAT CHANGED A SINGLE NATION- ME
I PETER 2:9

In July 2015, another event drastically impacted my life and helped me find the road back God. The first annual Breaking the Silence Conference was launched. This conference made a profound impact on my life, especially in the area of prayer. One of the speakers, Pastor Joshua, claimed that prayer changed the entire nation of Uganda. He spoke about prayer altars and the importance of consistency in prayer. He began telling us about the prayer altars they set up in every governmental office in Uganda and how they prayed every single day.

I was so taken by this topic that I started asking the Lord how this kind of prayer could change me—a single nation. I am a nation. In I Peter 2:9 (NLT), it says, "But you are not like that, for you are a chosen people. You are royal priests, a holy nation, God's very own possession. As a result, you can show others the goodness of God, for he called you out of the darkness into his wonderful light."

I understood consistency in prayer but setting up altars was a little more foreign to me. At the time, I was reading the Bible all the way through for a second time. This time I was seeing things I hadn't seen before. For example, every time God's people conquered new land, their first act was building some sort of altar to the Lord. This was to signify that this territory now belonged to God's people. I began to put this into practice in my life. Each time a battle was won in my life, I built an altar to let the enemy know that my fight in this area is over. From my second reading of the Word, I also realized that after a battle is fought and won, another battle that you didn't even know existed will pop up. You couldn't see it before because of the battle that was in front of it. It's kind of like peeling an onion, layer by layer; the process takes away one layer at a time.

I began to ask the Lord, what does having a more effective prayer life look like? His response to me: my prayers need to be more strategic and more specific. Before I was praying general and/or aimless prayers, which means I was praying things that God had already answered or things he couldn't answer. For instance, I would pray, "Father, be with me as I travel to Pueblo today for an interview." This prayer was amiss because His Word says in Hebrews 13:5 that He will never leave me nor forsake me. Instead, my prayer should have sounded like this, "Lord, thank You for being with me as I travel to Pueblo today for an interview." Psalm 90:17 says the favor of the Lord already rests upon me. Instead of praying, "Lord, give me favor for this job," I simply prayed, "Lord, thank You for Your favor that rests upon me." As a result of this kind of praying, I became more aware of the words coming out of my mouth and had more gratitude for the things I already possessed as a child in the kingdom.

At the conference, Pastor Joshua taught me that effective prayer was not based on the number of people at the meeting nor how long your prayer meeting lasted nor how many words were uttered. Effective prayer is consistent prayer. The Bible says to pray without ceasing and continually (I Thessalonians 5:17). Pray, even when you don't want to pray! Why? Prayer is a form of praise. When you pray, even when you don't want to initially, you have moved into the realm of offering up a sacrifice of praise through prayer. I have found that when that kind of prayer is offered up, it really makes the devil mad.

Speaking of making the devil mad, if you want to take your prayer life to a whole other level and move into some covert-operations warfare, begin to speak in your heavenly language. To begin with, the devil can't understand a word you're saying. More importantly, you will be praying with the Spirit, so you will pray perfect prayers.

Have you ever needed to pray for something and you didn't have the words? Begin to pray in your heavenly language because Romans 8:26-27 (ESV) tells us that the Holy Spirit "helps us in our weakness. For we do not know what to pray as we ought, but the Spirit himself intercedes for us with groanings too deep for words."

Prayer is the language of Heaven. Prayer is our reminder that humility is the way into the throne room. We can come boldly and with confidence (Hebrews 4:16), but, when we pray, we are acknowledging our dependency on the Father. We are admitting to God that we need His help. The Bible tells us that in our weakness, He is made strong (2 Corinthians 12:9, KJV).

First the Word and then prayer—the sword and the Spirit. They are the dynamic duo. I've been made alive, I am well, and I was made whole because of these precious gifts the Father has given me. They will forever be etched in my mind, on my heart and continually come out of my mouth.

CHAPTER VIII

DEVIL, INTERPRET THIS!
ROMANS 8:26-27

Romans 8:26-27 (KJV) states that, "Likewise the Spirit also helpeth our infirmities: for we know not what we should pray for as we ought: but the Spirit itself maketh intercession for us with groanings which cannot be uttered. And he that searcheth the hearts knoweth what is the mind of the Spirit, because he maketh intercession for the saints according to the will of God."

The Word was and still is a vital lifeline I use in my daily life. I would never give up reading or studying it for anything! It is my most prized possession. It truly brings me spiritual nourishment. While the Word played a very important role in guiding me back into fellowship with Father God, I have another weapon that when accompanied by the Word becomes an atomic bomb that literally disables the enemy completely from having any impact in my life at all! That weapon is prayer.

When you are in a relationship with someone, whether it's romantic, paternal, friendship or whatever, the way you build that relationship and cause it to grow is to spend time with that other person. Communicating or talking is also an essential ingredient in developing that relationship. It's no different in regards to our relationship with God the Father. We must spend time with Him, and we must communicate with Him. This is called prayer, which in simple terms means talking with God.

I believe there are many different ways to approach the Father in prayer, but we should always approach with honor, reverence and respect. Sometimes we come as children, who just want Him to be our daddy as we innocently and confidently sit before Him knowing He loves us. We get to watch Him lavish His love on us, and He never asks or expects anything in return. He's just glad you came.

Other times we may approach Him broken and weak. We have done all we know to do. We have prayed all the prayers we know to pray. We have prayed the Word, but we still cannot find the success we are seeking. The Word of God tells us that the enemy is very crafty and deceptive; he even used scripture to try to tempt Jesus by quoting bits and pieces out of context. The devil will use any means necessary to keep you from winning.

In Luke 24:49 (KJV), Jesus said, "And, behold, I send the promise of my Father upon you: but tarry ye in the city of Jerusalem, until ye be endued with power from on high." In Acts 1:4 (KJV) He "commanded them that they should not depart from Jerusalem, but wait for the promise of the Father, which, saith he, ye have heard of me." Later in verse 8 of the same chapter, Jesus said, "But ye shall receive power, after that the Holy Ghost is come upon you: and ye shall be witnesses unto me both in Jerusalem, and in all Judaea, and in Samaria, and unto the uttermost part of the earth." Later still in Acts 2:1-4, we read, "And when the day of Pentecost was fully come, they were all with one accord in one place. And suddenly there came a sound from heaven as of a rushing mighty wind, and it filled all the house where they were sitting. And there appeared unto them cloven tongues like as of fire, and it sat upon each of them. And they were all filled with the Holy Ghost, and began to speak with other tongues, as the Spirit gave them utterance." I mentioned this heavenly language in the previous chapter.

You and I can pray in our natural tongue, which people and the devil can understand; but, when you have been endued with power from on high, praying in the spirit in other tongues, the devil can't understand a single word you are saying. What this creates for the believer is a strategy that renders the enemy powerless in our affairs. Another benefit of speaking or praying in tongues is that you are not praying alone. There is a partnership; the Holy Spirit is praying with your spirit. Now your prayer becomes a perfect prayer because you are praying the will of God. The Word of God tells us in Romans 8 that the spirit makes intercession in accordance to the Will of God.

This is a game changer. First prayer and now prayer with the spirit; it's empowering and essential for victory over the evil one.

CHAPTER IX

PRE-MADE FOR GLORY

Ephesians 1:3-6 (NKJV) says, "Blessed be the God and Father of our Lord Jesus Christ, who has blessed us with every spiritual blessing in the heavenly places in Christ, just as He chose us in Him before the foundation of the world, that we should be holy and without blame before Him in love, having predestined us to adoption as sons by Jesus Christ to Himself, according to the good pleasure of His will, to the praise of the glory of His grace, by which He made us accepted in the Beloved." If ever I had a question about who I was or where I belonged or even what I was created for this passage of scripture just settle it once and for all.

As hard as the enemy tried, he could not pull me away from destiny. For four years, I ran away from my destiny. I made friendships with the world. I believed lies when I compromised my beliefs and began to doubt what God really said. I allowed carnality to creep into my DNA. I became that "frog in the kettle" who little by little accepted the lie that the lukewarm temperature of my atmosphere was normal. I became like the Laodicean church in Revelation 3:15-18 (NIV); "I know your deeds, that you are neither cold nor hot. I wish you were either one or the other! So, because you are lukewarm—neither hot nor cold—I am about to spit you out of my mouth. You say, 'I am rich; I have acquired wealth and do not need a thing.' But you do not realize that you are wretched, pitiful, poor, blind and naked. I counsel you to buy from me gold refined in the fire, so you can become rich; and white clothes to wear, so you can cover your shameful nakedness; and salve to put on your eyes, so you can see." Jesus reminded them that the answer to their dilemma was repentance. It was my answer too. I already belonged to God; repentance just got the ball rolling back into the right direction.

The odd thing about my season of running away from the Father was that I never found a place where I felt like I fit in. I always felt like a third wheel or the fifth man out. I was always uncomfortable about what I was doing or the places I found myself in. Later, I realized I was uncomfortable because the things I was doing and the places I ended up in were contrary to the nature that was inside of me. Because I was predestined before the foundation of the world to walk blameless before the Father, when I went against my destiny, it grieved Him and made Him very sad. Even though I participated in things that at the time seemed right in my eyes, it wasn't what I was supposed to be doing. I had taken an uncomfortable detour from my journey towards my destiny. Every day I would wake up and know there was more to life than this; at least, I hoped there was more.

Looking back, I can recall times I tried to break into arenas of sin that were very dark but I couldn't fully enter in. At the time, I wasn't sure what it was that kept me at bay. At times, it felt like there were boundaries set up around me. It was like there was this line that I was not allowed to go beyond. When I tried to enter sin anyway, people would say things like, "What are you doing here? You don't even belong here. You seem out of place. How did you even get as far as you did?" I kept banging on the door of darkness, and it just wouldn't let me in.

Later I realized this was the grace of my Father in my life. He protected me from pure darkness knowing that my going through those closed doors would have possibly cost me my eternal life. As a result of the Father's shield, many of my plans were frustrated, and many relationships went awry for no particular reason.

Things just began to blow up, but it was all part of the Father's plan to point me back in the direction of my true identity. This, in turn, would lead me to my destiny.

Have you ever had spiritual conversations with friends even while you're in the midst of activities of darkness? I think the reason why that can happen is because the Father is willing to come to us and meet us right where we are at. If we chose to, we could take His hand, and He would lead us right out. He did allow His Son to die for me over two thousand years ago with no guarantee that I was going to accept Him and live for Him in the future.

I believe the most sobering part of this whole adventure is found in Proverbs 16:4 (NLT) where it says, "The LORD has made everything for his own purposes, even the wicked for a day of disaster." The thought that stuck me was that I could have been one of those created wicked, destined to live in eternity apart from my Father. I thought about Judas Iscariot who ultimately betrayed Jesus because he chose not to deal with his heart, which was the foundation of his wickedness. This is why we can never trust our heart apart from God to make any decision. The Bible says, "The heart is deceitful above all things, and desperately wicked: who can know it?" (Jeremiah 17:9, KJV)).

Remember earlier when I alluded to my heart being as hard as rock? If it had not been for the Word of God that softened and enlightened my heart, my decisions in life would have always been made from wicked intentions. On the day of accountability, I would have been held accountable for that wickedness.

Guard your heart by guarding your mind and never step out of the guidance and protection of the Word of God

CHAPTER X

GET TO CLASS
HEBREWS 10:24-25

I think one of the biggest deceptions from the enemy is the idea that they are the only ones going through what they are going through. As a result of this mindset, he is very successful in causing us to isolate. He understands, as all predators do, that you're an easy prey if you are left alone. In I Peter 4:12 (NKJV), we read, "Beloved, do not think it strange concerning the fiery trial which is to try you, as though some strange thing happened to you." You're not the only one! Thank God for scripture that unravels this lie and lets us in on the real truth.

I am an advocate of aloneness. If it is a season for you to seek the Father for answers, and you are attempting to shut out the voices of this world so you hear clearly, that's an entirely different set of circumstances. However, being alone to suffer in silence is not okay. In Ecclesiastes 4:9-10 (NLT), it says, "Two people are better off than one, for they can help each other succeed. If one person falls, the other can reach out and help. But someone who falls alone is in real trouble." We were never designed to be alone, always for relationships.

For about one year, I sought aloneness because I needed everything and everybody to shut up. I didn't trust anyone. I didn't believe anything that anybody said. I had built up walls so high I couldn't get out and absolutely no one was getting in. I didn't know what the truth was anymore. The only truth I knew all turned out to be deception.

I eventually started going back to church after the first Breaking the Silence Conference. I would slip in right before service started and I would slip out right before it ended. I had no desire nor any intention of speaking to anyone about anything. I didn't want to get close to anyone, and I didn't want anyone close to me.

When I was in church services I was like a sponge. I was so hungry for truth that I pulled on the anointing of the speaker to such a degree that they preached a different message from what they had prepared. How do I know this? Because they would make comments like, "I'm not sure where that came from, but somebody in here needed it." I believe many times Father did that just for me. I believe He satisfied my hunger.

I remember one time a guest speaker came in unexpectedly. Our pastor asked him to bring a word of greeting to the congregation. The greeting he bought was a key to something I was seeking the Father about. I felt stuck, but He uttered a few words that unlocked the revelation I needed to move on. He said, "You have done all you can do. There is no more. Allow the Lord to now do what He needs to do." At those words, a peace fell over me and the constant desire to do more left me. I committed this thing to the Lord and left it alone; the next day it was settled.

Another time, I was sitting in service and praying through some things to get some answers from the Lord. Then my pastor said one word. This word caused a series of events that set me free from an offense that had caused me to harbor bitterness and resentment for over five years. It was something I thought I had dealt with in years gone by, but for some reason it kept resurfacing. I really wasn't sure what I needed to do to settle this in my heart until I heard the word *forgive*. I prayed to the Lord to make a way for a meeting. He orchestrated it in about twenty-four hours. As I sat in the office and began to share and forgive, I could feel these weights being lifted off of me, one by one, until they were all gone.

One week, my pastor started a series on the Armor of God. I listened to every single word of this series, but I wasn't ready to receive it yet. It was a premature word for the season I was in, but I knew it would be used for a later season in my life. Even in my blindness, I knew that without the loin belt to hold them all in place, this armor would be of no use to me.

The foundation and the piece that holds all the other pieces together is the loin belt of truth. I was searching for truth, and I continued my journey to the truth over the next year. All I wanted to know was what God said about any issue; if it didn't line up with what Father God was saying, I wanted no part.

Hebrews 10:24-25 (NLT) says, "Let us think of ways to motivate one another to acts of love and good works. And let us not neglect our meeting together, as some people do, but encourage one another, especially now that the day of his return is drawing near." In light of this verse, I often heard the phrase "Get to class." When I contemplated staying home from church or any other Christian gathering, I would hear these words. Father was always trying to give me answers, but, if I had stayed at home, I'd have missed it. My exhortation to you is this: don't let another week go by and assemble together with people who speak the truth of the Word of God.

CHAPTER XI

HARVEST VS MIRACLE

"Get into God's economy. I'd rather live off the harvest then live off a miracle." These were the words I heard often from the pulpit of my church.

In chapter one, I asked God the questions: "What do I need to do to see Your face again? How do I hear Your voice again?" God shared with me that I needed to read the Letter He sent me; so, I did. As I continued to read His Word, I realized that prayer was also needed to rebuild my intimate relationship with my Father. Now, He revealed to me yet another piece I needed to return to Him. His desire was to have me back on all levels.

Malachi 3:7-12 (AMP) reads:

> "Yet from the days of your fathers you have turned away from My statutes *and* ordinances and have not kept them. Return to Me, and I will return to you," says the LORD of hosts. "But you say, 'How shall we return?'

> "Will a man rob God? Yet you are robbing Me! But you say, 'In what way have we robbed You?' In tithes and offerings [you have withheld]. You are cursed with a curse, for you are robbing Me, this whole nation! Bring all the tithes (the tenth)

into the storehouse, so that there may be food in My house, and test Me now in this," says the LORD of hosts, "if I will not open for you the windows of heaven and pour out for you [so great] a blessing until there is no more room to receive it. Then I will rebuke the devourer (insects, plague) for your sake and he will not destroy the fruits of the ground, nor will your vine in the field drop *its grapes* [before harvest]," says the Lord of hosts. "All nations shall call you happy *and* blessed, for you shall be a land of delight," says the LORD of hosts.

Money has always been a source of contention and a deep wound for me. I never had enough of it. There was never enough to make ends meet. At this stage of my life, I was a single parent trying to take care of three kids. I admit I spent my money on foolish habits I had picked up the last four years; but, it was more than that. It felt like it was always going to be this way. I later found out it was a generational curse I had never been set free from.

I kept hearing my pastor say to get into "God's economy" where it's safe. He talked about how the economy of this world is failing and you can't trust it. He said the only economy that you can trust in is God's. I knew I had to learn how to move over to God's economy and do things His way. Father also told me this was another way I could come back to Him. He said, "Not only do you get to see My face again, but You get to see My hand move on your behalf. I want to show you all my goodness, Mary."

I began to tithe and give into the work of the Kingdom. I remember the first Sunday I gave. The enemy harassed me up until I let go of the envelope and dropped it into the offering bucket. When you deal with a spirit of lack, it's not easy to trust that if you put $220 in an offering bucket it will rebuke the devourer. This was not an easy thing for me to do. This took a lot of faith and all the trust I had inside me to be obedient and do what He was telling me to do. I knew I wanted to get back to Him and tithing was another area in my life that I had robbed God, because I was taking what was rightfully His. Besides, I needed to be able to see His face again. I didn't want anything to come between us ever.

This was possibly the hardest area of my life to surrender to God simply because of fear. I mean the kind of fear that makes you sick with worry. You see, I didn't understand how sowing and reaping really worked. I didn't understand that what I give I will always get back. For example, If I give love, I will get love back. If I gave friendship, I got friendship back. On the contrary, what I didn't give, I didn't get back.

Needless to say, this is something I had to work through and it took time. I will tell you though, even after tithing for over two years, the enemy returned with the same deception and caused me to question God again. Fear gripped me, and I bought the lie that Father was not going to open the windows of heaven and pour out a blessing. I forgot what He had done for the last two years. For two pay cycles (about a month), this battle went on inside me. The fear was so intense that I held on to the portion I was going to give for about a week during the second pay cycle. I just kept it. I didn't give it. I didn't spend it. Then, for the first time in two years, I talked with a fellow believer and shared with them what was going on inside me. What they said to me was so profound. Very boldly and sternly, she told me, "Release the tithe, because you don't need the guilt and shame of not giving compounded with the way you already feel." That night I poured out my heart to Father. I told Him I did not have the faith required to give this money. I told him I was scared. Finally, I gave the tithe. I believe that act of faith, even in my unbelief, broke the enemy's back that day. For those who are wondering—all the things I needed to take care of my family were supplied. Actually, it was taken care of in abundance.

Living in harvest is a fruit of sowing and giving. It is certainly more pleasurable to live in harvest than it is to live a life of needing a miracle every month. Now the Father requires even more from me than a simple tithe, because to whom much is given much is required.

CHAPTER XII

THE YELLOW ROPE

I saw a demonstration on Youtube that rocked my world. This pastor was holding a long, thick rope. The length of the rope represented eternity. He had painted a portion of the rope, around 8 to 10 inches, the color yellow. He held the yellow portion of the rope in the air and asked this question: "Is what you're holding onto right now worth all eternity?" This question blew me away.

The yellow portion of the rope represented my lifetime of about ninety years. The rest of the rope, which was so long I couldn't see all of it because it was hidden off stage behind the curtains, represented eternity. It was ninety years compared to eternity.

I began searching my heart for those things I knew I needed to let go of. Even though I wasn't practicing or participating in questionable activities, my heart still needed to let go of some things. When I saw this clip on Youtube, it brought my life into perspective. There had been a time in my life that I was so far away from God that I would have willingly chose to continue in my sin for the next 40 or 50 years and go to hell for eternity rather than choose Jesus. This is how blind I was and how dark my mind had gotten. This is how far away from the truth I had wandered. Was this short season of sin worth going to hell for?

I needed to make a choice. Most of my friends who were walking with the Lord thought this was a no brainer. "Heaven over hell? You got this, Mary!" they would say. But did I? Sin is real and it is fun for a time. Anyone who tells you it isn't needs to repent for lying. Love is love, even when it is not of God. A broken heart still hurts even if it's from an ungodly relationship. It's true when psychology says the mind cannot tell the difference between real and fantasy. I know because I couldn't tell the difference.

I wrestled with this for many months. What I really needed to do was settle some things once and for all in my heart. I had to think eternally, and I had to see the kingdom in a different way. I had to be reminded of my purpose and what I was created for. I had to remember the things I had read in the Letter and how my Father God was desperately trying to get me back ever since the fall of mankind in the garden. I had to remember He predestined me to be His since the foundation of the world. I had to remember that He sent His son to die for me two-thousand years ago to bring me back into right relationship with Him. I had to remember He died a brutal death and that He rose from the grave and descended into hell then ascended into heaven to go and prepare a place for me. I had to remember that He's coming back soon to get me. I had to remember He was looking forward to spending eternity with me. I had to remember I am His child and He is my Father. I had to remember what was in my hands was not worth spending eternity in hell. I had to let go once and for all in order to be free.

PART 2
CHAINED TO THE TRUTH

CHAPTER I

INTRODUCTION

No one wants to be lied to. No one wants to live their life where they are always on the guard. Who wants to live a life where you have your walls up so high you can't even see out, let alone let anyone in? Everybody needs somebody or something they can trust and rely on. Everybody needs someone who believes in them even when they don't believe in themselves. I believe people want to know primarily three things: Who am I? Why am I here? and What is my purpose? We need to understand that this thing we call life is all bigger than us. We need to know there is an eternal purpose. There has to be more than this. People search but have no idea what they are searching for; if they find it, they won't even realize it.

I know I was searching hard and long. I was searching to the point of that if something didn't change I wanted God to take me home. I had to have more. I needed to know there was more to life than this. Everywhere I looked, no matter if it was in the world or in the church, I wasn't finding what I was looking for. Nothing was real. Nothing was tangible for me. All was vanity, as Solomon put it so clearly (Ecclesiastes 1:14, ESV). He was tired of it all. Tired of the "rat race."

I was tired of the masks people put on (and some put on pretty good faces). It is a ridiculous misconception for a person to think that they are the only ones hurting and no one else is going through something or has ever gone through what they are facing right now. I Peter 5:9 (NLT) says, "Stand firm against him, and be strong in your faith. Remember that your family of believers all over the world is going through the same kind of suffering you are."

Silent suffering is an epidemic. We live in a world where there is no trust because truth is always changing. People cope with what life brings them the best way they can. I believe this is okay in certain seasons of our lives until we know better. For example, I have learned that community is vital. We were not created to do things all alone. With aloneness comes two things: first, you have no help if you fall; second, there is no accountability. In Ecclesiastes 4:10 (NIV), it says, "If either of them falls down, one can help the other up. But pity anyone who falls and has no one to help them up." In Proverbs 15:22 (NLT), it says, "Plans go wrong for lack of advice; many advisers bring success." Proverbs 11:14 (KJV) tells us, "Where no counsel is, the people fall: but in the multitude of counselors there is safety."

It is true you must be very selective about where your counsel comes from. I have one source for the truth that is allowed to influence my life and that is the infallible Word of God. I don't say this because it sounds like something a Christian is supposed to say. I say this because for me, it's the absolute truth. I saw this work first hand in my life. It was the key that lead me to the path of life.

In this section, I will reveal three things in my life that caused me to come to the conclusion that *Chained to the Truth* is where I will always be; those three things are the source, power, and persuasion. If we must be slaves to something, why not be slaves to the truth? I decided this is the way it's going to be for me. I will tell you one thing: I have never been so free as I am today!

CHAPTER II

SOURCE OF TRUTH

Your truth will only be as real as the source of your truth. How reliable is your source? How often does your source change the truth? Does your truth change with circumstances or with the social climate? Can you confidently say that your source has always given you the appropriate answer to every question or circumstance you have ever faced? Has your source ever let you down? We all have sources we have used or are using, whether they are people, books, beliefs, etc. What I want to share with you is my experience and the infallible truth that I have come to know and trust.

My source has proved itself tried and true time and time again. My source is the Word of God. This is the standard I use to compare everything in my life against. When faced with an obstacle, a question or a decision, I look to the Word to guide me to the answer. My moral thermometer is based on what the Word says and not on the changing world around me. For example, the Bible says it's not what goes into a man that defiles him but it's what comes out of him (Mark 7:20-23). What's in your heart is what comes out. In my younger years, I worked at UPS as a preloader. I was the person who loaded the truck in the wee hours of the morning. I worked with a bunch of young guys and every other word out of their mouth was profanity. They told me time and time again that after a few months on the job I would start cussing too. I confidently told them it would never happen, because I knew that it wasn't in me so it couldn't come out of me. Honestly, it never did, and I worked there for about a year.

The Bible says, "Do not be deceived: 'Bad company ruins good morals'" (1 Corinthians 15:33, ESV). I have to be conscious about who I hang out with. Another scripture says you will become like those you hang around with (Proverbs 13:20). This does not just pertain to the bad influences but the good ones as well. I made a choice to hang around with those who would propel me into my destiny as opposed to keeping me from it. 2 Corinthians 6:17 tells me to come out from among unbelievers and be separate. You wouldn't spend all your time with a person who loves a different football team than you do. Why? Because you would spend most of your time together trying to convince the other one that your team is better instead of enjoying each other's company and the game. An even better example would be in the arena of politics: Democrat vs Republican. There is no difference if you are speaking in the spiritual arena. If you as a believer spent the majority of your time with unbelievers you would constantly oppose one another instead of enjoying the fellowship. Furthermore, the Bible says, "No one who is born of God will continue to sin, because God's seed remains in them; they cannot go on sinning, because they have been born of God" (1 John 3:9, NIV).

Here is a practical example of how to align your life with the Word. The way I treat my money is based on the truth of the Word. The Word informs how I give it away, how I save it and how I spend it. Here are two truths that keep me on the right path: tithing and leaving an inheritance. Proverbs 3:9 (NIV) says to honor the Lord with your wealth and first fruits. I am a believer in the tithe (which means I give 10% of my increase) to my local church. Previously, I mentioned my pastor who talked about God's economy, and how if we are in His economy we will always be cared for no matter what the economy around us is doing. That stuck with me and I came to find it to be very true in my life. I also saw this play out in the lives of those around me who did the same. The Bible promises in Matthew 6:33 (NIV) that if we "seek first his kingdom and his righteousness, and all these things will be given to you as well." I learned "all these things" meant my needs and my wants. I had been working so hard to acquire these things. If I did it the right way, I would have them anyway. Proverbs 13:22 (NIV) says, "A good person leaves an inheritance for their children's children." That is my goal. Keep in mind, though, that you cannot leave an inheritance for your grandchildren if you haven't been wise with your own.

If I have decisions to make or problems I need to solve, James 1:5 (NIV) says, "If any of you lacks wisdom, you should ask God, who gives generously to all without finding fault, and it will be given to you." This means it doesn't matter who you are; He is waiting to give you the strategies and knowledge that you need to make your way successful.

If I have questions about my health (what to eat), 1 Corinthians 6:12 (AMP) says, "Everything is permissible for me, but not all things are beneficial." Later in verse 20, it says, "You were bought with a price [you were actually purchased with the precious blood of Jesus and made His own]. So then, honor *and* glorify God with your body." Romans 12:1 (ESV) tells us "to present your bodies as a living sacrifice, holy and acceptable to God." Lastly, 3 John 2 says, "Beloved, I wish above all things that thou mayest prosper and be in health, even as thy soul prospereth." Your soul speaks of your mind, your will and your emotions. The foods I eat and the effect these foods have on my body should align with the wisdom of the Word.

What is the truth? In John 14:6 (NIV), it says, "Jesus answered, 'I am the way and the truth and the life. No one comes to the Father except through me.'" In John 17:17 (NIV), it says, "Sanctify them by the truth; your word is truth." I know without any doubt in my mind that God's word is the truth I must live by. Without fail,

God's word has given me everything I have needed—answers, encouragement, wisdom or light in my darkest times. It has never turned me away without satisfying my every want or need. I am forever chained to the truth.

Does truth matter? In my life it did, and it still does. It made a difference in the choices I made. In order to make wise decisions that benefited my well-being, I needed the truth. Now before I can go on, I want to address deception. Deception is nothing new under the sun. Deception is so close to the truth because it contains some truth. It made its way right into the Garden of Eden. It's as old as mankind.

Deception always begins with a question. In Genesis 3 (ESV), the serpent began his scheme with, "Did God actually say?" Then, deception continues its path with reason that hooks your curiosity. Next the serpent begins to give his interpretation of what God meant when He said, "but of the tree of the knowledge of good and evil you shall not eat, for in the day that you eat of it you sall surely die" (Genesis 2:17). The serpent said, "You will not surely die. For God knows that when you eat of it your eyes will be opened, and you will be like God, knowing good from evil" (Genesis 3:4-5). Eve was presented with a question, and that's all that was needed for her to engage in this conversation that would ultimately convince her to believe the lie that God was holding out on her and Adam. Then seeing that the fruit was good for eating, she ate. Then Adam ate, and thus began the downward spiral of mankind.

In my case it was no different. I knew the truth, and what it said. My deception began as a result of an offense against those that I loved and honored. These were people I looked up to and respected. I had so many blinders on I couldn't even see the pot shots the enemy had planned for me. I was already fed up with people in the church and the many masks they wore Sunday after Sunday. I was tired of the pretense and the fake lives they were living. In hindsight, I can see that this was only characteristic of a few, but the enemy knew what few to allow to cross my path. He knew I was done and this would be the last straw for me to walk away and turn my back not only on the church but on God himself.

We live in a society where we accept alternative everything: alternative medicine, alternative sweeteners, alternative lifestyles. Why not alternative truth? Alternative means to exist outside of what was originally established. For example, there is pharmaceutical medicine as opposed to natural medicine, or the original heterosexual makeup of the family as opposed to the alternative lifestyle of same sex marriage. Just like a lie, if you hear alternatives long enough, you begin to believe them as a way of life and before you know it everything becomes ok. We no longer have any standards to live by; every man becomes right in his own eyes. The Bible warns us in Proverbs 14:12 (NIV) when it says, "There is a way that appears to be right, but in the end it leads to death." I was a person who was led by my heart which was not a good thing to follow because the Bible tells me in Jeremiah 17:9 (NKJV), "The heart *is* deceitful above all *things*, And desperately wicked; Who can know it?" In Proverbs 4:23 (ESV) it instructs me to "Keep your heart with all vigilance, for from it flow the springs of life." Living by my heart made me very unstable and it caused me to have no boundaries or restrictions in life. The more unstable I became, the easier it was for blindness to set in. After years of this my end result was double-mindedness. From day to day, my truth changed. My boundaries became larger and larger. The rules of the game changed constantly. I found myself treating everything as truth. I allowed the unthinkable into my heart and allowed it to play out in my life. I started to become someone I really wasn't because "as he thinks in his heart, so is he" (Proverbs 23:7, AMP). As I thought wrong, I began to act wrong.

Does truth matter? It certainly did in my life. The untruths lead me down a road of endless frustration and striving for possessions that added to my self-destruction rather than expand my self-worth. The untruths drew me away from the only one who expressed genuine care and unconditional love for me. John 3:16 reveals that God so loved the world that He gave His only begotten son Jesus to die on a cross for me. God put truth here, hoping I would search it out and find meaning and purpose in the land of the living. Truth is essential to living well like air is essential to breathing. It's as simple as life and death. The Bible says in Deuteronomy 30:19 (NKJV), "I have set before you life and death, blessing and cursing; therefore choose life, that both you and your descendants may live."

What is the reason for truth? Truth, according to dictionary. com, allows us to form conclusions, judgments, or inferences from facts or premises. 2 Timothy 3:16 (KJV) tells us that, "All scripture is given by inspiration of God, and is profitable for doctrine, for reproof, for correction, for instruction in righteousness."

The first thing that 2 Timothy brings out is that scripture is profitable. It's beneficial and useful, and not just a bunch of words on a page in a book. When something is useful it serves a purpose. It meets a need. It solves a problem. Our problem is an unrenewed mind. The Word of God equips us. It teaches us the knowledge and skills to enable us to conduct ourselves in a manner worthy of repeating. We are all leaders. People are watching your every move and listening to every word being spoken.

Next, 2 Timothy says the Word of God is for reproof. In my classroom, I often use a KWL chart (what do you know, what do you want to know, what did you learn). This chart informs me about the level of background knowledge of my class. The K denotes what they already know. With the W, they write down questions as to what they want to know. With the L, they are to reflect on what they learned.

The word reproof is like the KWL chart. First, the Word of God judges your level of the knowledge of the truth. My unrenewed mind had to be totally renovated because I had drifted far from the truth and into deception. I had half-truths, which

I believe made things even worse because I had to be untaught before I could really grasp and absorb the pure truth. Judging usually carries a negative connotation, especially when people are involved in the judging. In 2 Samuel 24:14 (NIV), "David said to Gad, 'I am in deep distress. Let us fall into the hands of the LORD, for his mercy is great; but do not let me fall into human hands.'" In Psalm 9:8 (ESV) it declares, "he judges the world with righteousness; he judges the peoples with uprightness." Paul tells us, "There is therefore now no condemnation for those who are in Christ Jesus" (Romans 8:1). If you are in the truth, you are in Christ Jesus. John 3:17 reminds us that "God did not send his Son into the world to condemn the world, but in order that the world might be saved through him." I'll take God's judgment any day of the week.

After it reproofs, truth corrects. I am a teacher at heart. I love to use every moment as a teaching moment. When I correct, it's not simply to draw attention to inappropriate behavior; it's my responsibility to correct the wrong so that it doesn't happen as often anymore. Eventually, I hope that the behavior is extinguished because the truth was taught.

Correction is meant to be something that is substituted to revise what is wrong or inaccurate. In my class we have a writing process we use to make scholars better writers. It's usually the step we spend the most time on. The kids hate it because they are rewriting and rewriting and rewriting to make a good essay the best it can be. Some of them don't even like to rewrite one time. They would rather settle for the lesser grade. Sadly, we do the same thing when we settle for half-truths rather than the absolute truth because of the fear of offending.

Paul asks, "Have I become your enemy by telling you the truth?" (Galatians 4:16, ESV). Jesus asks, "Do you think that I have come to give peace on earth? No, I tell you, but rather division" (Luke 12:51, ESV). The reason truth brings division is because many do not desire the pure truth. They would rather have a little truth and a little lie so they blend more easily with culture. The truth is: truth will separate you from the crowd. We must ask ourselves: do we want to fit into culture and accept mediocrity, or do we want to impact culture and experience the fullness of why we exist?

The result of this process is to be trained in rightness. I often become frustrated when I get help from a "professional" and they do their job wrong which causes me further harm. I'll give you a real-life example. I ordered a bathing suit from a catalog and sadly had to return it for a different size. The lady on the phone asked me if I wanted to upgrade my credit card so I could shop at multiple stores instead of just one store. I said, "Sure. Why not?" Rather than making the exchange on the old card, she charged me on the new card for a new suit. When I got the new card in the mail, it already had a balance and I hadn't even used it yet. I went through customer service and got it all straightened out, but it cost me time I didn't have on the phone trying to make a wrong right. Apparently, she needed more training. The whole premise behind truth is to train you up to do the right thing with a pure heart. I now experience this on a daily basis. I don't have to think really hard about what the right thing is in any given situation because now I know the truth. It's not based on what people James 4:17 (NKJV) says, "Therefore, to him who knows to do good and does not do *it*, to him it is sin." I never want to be found doing something wrong on purpose. That's a dead-end road. These are a few reasons why truth is the better road.

CHAPTER III
POWER OF TRUTH (WORD)

The truth for me is the Word of God. I am going to take it to the next level and reveal to you that the Word of God is referring to Jesus. In the John 1:1 (AMP). it reads, "In the beginning [before all time] was the Word (Christ), and the Word was with God, and the Word was God Himself." Later in John 1:14, it says, "And the Word (Christ) became flesh, and lived among us; and we [actually] saw His glory, glory as belongs to the [One and] only begotten *Son* of the Father, [the Son who is truly unique, the only One of His kind, who is] full of grace and truth (absolutely free of deception)." In this next section, I want to help you discover through my experiences the amazing power of this word in the man of Jesus.

I discovered very quickly that the Word can save you when nothing or no one else can. People, friends, and even mentors tried to encourage me on my journey of getting back into right relationship with the Lord, but all to no avail. It was the encounter with the Father himself that told me what to do. Paul had an encounter with the Lord on the road to Damascus (Acts 9). He was on his way to kill more Christians but the Lord had other plans for him. The Lord met Paul and ultimately gave him an invitation to go to the gentiles and tell them the good news of the gospel. In my Damascus-road experience, I was invited to simply read the Word but that was a life-changing experience. I can honestly say it was the thing that saved me from continuing down the road of destruction. James 1:21 (AMP), simply puts it, "So get rid of all uncleanness and all that remains of wickedness, and with a humble spirit receive the word [of God] which is implanted [actually rooted in your heart], which is able to save your souls." I had to come to that point where I had to receive the Word in order for its power to work in my life. I am so glad I accepted the invitation of the Holy Spirit to just read. The Word has the power to save.

Now as believers, we refer to Jesus as God in the flesh, and the Holy Spirit as God in the spirit. The Holy Trinity is God the Father, God the Son and the God Holy Spirit, three in one. If Jesus is the Word in flesh, then the Holy spirit would be the Word in spirit. During this season in my life, I was trying to get back to God, but I had no clue where to begin. John 16:13 (AMP) says, "But when He, the Spirit of Truth, comes, He will guide you into all the truth (full and complete truth). For He will not speak on His own initiative, but He will speak whatever He hears [from the Father—the message regarding the Son], and He will disclose to you what is to come [in the future]." The Word had the power to guide me in all truth—to literally bring me back into the right fellowship with a living God. The Word also began to share with me things to come in my life. Jeremiah 29:11 (AMP) says, "'For I know the plans *and* thoughts that I have for you,' says the Lord, 'plans for peace *and* well-being and not for disaster, to give you a future and a hope.'"

The Word has the power to guide. The love of Jesus is unconditional but I found out quickly His promises were not. Often His promises would begin with "If you...Then I". One great illustration is in Matthew 6:33 (KJV) where Jesus says, "But seek ye first the Kingdom of God, and his righteousness; and all these things shall be added unto you." Another example is in Psalm 37:4 (KJV) which says, "Delight thyself also in the Lord: and he shall give thee the desires of thine heart." In Proverbs

3:5-6 (KJV) the Word says, "Trust in the LORD with all thine heart; and lean not unto thine own understanding. In all thy ways acknowledge him, and he shall direct thy paths." I had to learn to surrender my will, my heart and my mind and trust that his way was better.

The Word has the power to set you free. In John 8:31-32 (AMP), it says, "Jesus was saying to the Jews who had believed Him, 'If you abide in My word [continually obeying My teachings and living in accordance with them, then] you are truly My disciples. And you will know the truth [regarding salvation], and the truth will set you free [from the penalty of sin].'" In Romans 6:20-22 (NLT), it says, "When you were slaves to sin, you were free from the obligation to do right. And what was the result? You are now ashamed of the things you used to do, things that end in eternal doom. But now you are free from the power of sin and have become slaves of God. Now you do those things that lead to holiness and result in eternal life."

This scripture was by the far the one that made the most impact on my life. At times when I was away from the Lord, it seemed like the more I tried to do good, the more bad I wanted to do. I would not only do the bad thing I didn't want to do, but I would also take it to the next level. It was like I was pulled by a force that drove me to go farther and farther into darkness. I found out later that this was a power that was greater than I was apart from the truth. I failed because I was trying to fight this thing in my own strength. It was the power of sin. When I received the truth of the Word into my heart, it came alive in me. Then I believed what I John 4:4 (AMP), which says, "He who is in you is greater than he (Satan) who is in the world [of sinful mankind]." My greatest struggle was breaking free from the power of sin. Once I surrendered, it was just an exchange of God's will for mine. The Word has the power to set free. Romans 12:2 (AMP):

> Do not be conformed to this world [any longer
> with its superficial values and customs], but be
> transformed *and* progressively changed [as you
> mature spiritually] by the renewing of your mind
> [focusing on godly values and ethical attitudes], so
> that you may prove [for yourselves] what the will
> of God is, that which is good and acceptable and
> perfect [in His plan and purpose for you].

This was a truth that mobilized my mind into action which in turn propelled me into a whole new paradigm. I no longer had to conform to the world's system when it came to making decisions. I no longer had to submit to their values and ethics. I no longer had to care what they thought about me. I no longer had to be politically correct. I could now make choices based on biblical convictions. What a difference!

As I began to learn the truth, I found there was a different set of rules—a different way to do things and a different way to live. It's a way that counts for more than just the moment or just the here and now; it's an *eternal* way of life. When you renew your mind according to the Word, you become eternity-minded. You become harvest-minded because you become aware it's no longer just about you. In the garden of Gethsemane, when Jesus said, "everything is possible for you. Take this cup from me. Yet, not what I will, but what you will" (Mark 14:36, NIV). He knew His purpose had always been for the sake of my eternal wellbeing. One indicator that your mind has been renewed is when start seeing things from an eternal perspective. The Word has power to renew the mind.

During my journey on the road back to God, I knew there were a lot of people I had to forgive. I had to let the offenses go so I could be free. Talk about dying to the flesh. My pastor always talked about a seed. As the Bible says, "unless a kernel of wheat falls to the ground and dies, it remains only a single seed. But if it dies, it produces many seeds" (John 12:24, NIV). I had to forgive stupid, petty things. I had to do it because these stupid petty things were keeping me locked up in a prison of unforgiveness on a floor of bitterness. I had become so apathetic about everything. I just didn't care. Nothing mattered. I think I knew exactly how Solomon felt in Ecclesiastes. He in his older days had concluded that everything was pointless. Living really wasn't even that important to me anymore. On my journey through the Word, I came across many scriptures that talked about forgiveness. One that really tugged on my heart was Matthew 6:14-15 (AMP), "For if you forgive others their trespasses [their reckless and willful sins], your heavenly Father will also forgive you. But if you do not forgive others [nurturing your hurt and anger with the result that it interferes with your relationship with God], then your Father will not forgive your trespasses." That was a hard thing to wrap my mind around. I thought, "Nope, they hurt me so bad, they don't deserve to be forgiven. They knew better than to treat me that way. Besides, these people are in leadership in a church." Yet I kept seeing it in black and white on the pages of my Bible. It says, "For if you forgive other people when they sin against you, your heavenly Father will also forgive you. But if you do not forgive others their sins, your Father will not forgive your sins" (Matthew 6:14-15, NIV).

I not only needed to forgive but I needed to be forgiven. I also needed to be healed. I had neither the power nor the ability to do either one. I was helpless. I asked the Lord how I could forgive when my heart was so hard and broken? I thought, "Vulnerability is what put me in this predicament in the first place. I trusted, but then You allowed them to hurt me." Then I heard the Holy Spirit say, "Love covers a multitude of sins" (1 Peter 4:8, NLT). Hatred stirs up conflict, but love covers offenses (Proverbs 10:12, ESV). With these words, I knew the Lord was setting me up for the healing I needed, and it would start with forgiveness. I contemplated: do I want to love or hate? Do I want to stir up or cover up? Hatred looks for a fight, but love looks for someone to forgive. I was so tired of fighting even if it was against myself.

I am convinced the reason why this was so difficult at first was because the first person I had to forgive was myself. Until I could forgive myself, I couldn't forgive others. Then Holy Spirit said, "While you were yet a sinner, I died for you" (Romans 5:8). I heard Him say, "Because I forgave you, you can forgive yourself. I live in you and I am love; therefore, you are love. You are made in My image." Love covers a multitude of sins. Love keeps no record of wrongs (I Corinthians 13:5). The Word has power to forgive.

CHAPTER IV

PERSUADED BY TRUTH

John 2:13-17 (NIV) reads:

> When it was almost time for the Jewish Passover, Jesus went up to Jerusalem. In the temple courts he found people selling cattle, sheep and doves, and others sitting at tables exchanging money. So he made a whip out of cords, and drove all from the temple courts, both sheep and cattle; he scattered the coins of the money changers and overturned their tables. To those who sold doves he said, "Get these out of here! Stop turning my Father's house into a market!" His disciples remembered that it is written: "Zeal for your house will consume me."

Before the New Testament God abided *with* us. God walked with Abraham, Moses, Noah, David, Job and the prophets of the day. His dwelling place was in the Holy of Holies on Mount Sinai in the cloud by day and the fire by night. After Jesus was born, crucified and raised from the dead, the Spirit of God abides *in* us as believers. We are now His dwelling place. Just as Jesus displayed holy and righteous anger when he rebuked the Jewish people who were turning God's house (temple) into a house of thieves, we should be just as zealous about our temple which happens to be our body. We should not allow it to become a den for thieves or a place for sin to take up residence.

My question for you is this: are you going to allow this zealous Savior, who purchased you with His blood, to come in with His truth and grace to drive out the money changers of your life, scatter the mammon and overturn the tables on sin in order to make room for His precious Holy Spirit? If so, then I urge you, like Timothy was urged in 1 Timothy 6:20-21 (NIV), "guard what has been entrusted to your care. Turn away from godless chatter and the opposing ideas of what is falsely called knowledge, which some have professed and in so doing have departed from the faith."

Once you have said yes to the above, it's time to get practical. James 2:17 (NIV) says, "faith by itself, if it is not accompanied by action, is dead." I had to put some practical actions in place. In order for me to continue to be persuaded, I ensured these four things became a part of my daily life: 1) Time in the Word, 2) Time in prayer, 3) Guarding the words that came out of my mouth, and 4) Declaring "It is finished" to the enemy.

Psalms 1:2-3 (NIV) says:

> but whose delight is in the law of the LORD, and who meditates on his law day and night.
> That person is like a tree planted by streams of water, which yields its fruit in season and whose leaf does not wither—whatever they do prospers.

You may wonder how you can meditate on His Word day and night. Good question! I'm glad you asked. I learned to meditate on His word day and night by making sure I read the word before I went to bed every night. I believe your natural mind usually shuts down and sleeps, but your spirit man never sleeps. Psalm 121:2-4 (KJV) says, "My help cometh from the LORD, which made heaven and earth. He will not suffer thy foot to be moved: he that keepeth thee will not slumber. Behold, he that keepeth Israel shall neither slumber nor sleep."

I believe my spirit was communing with the Holy Spirit all night long. I believe each word was woven into the fabric of my being while I slept. When I awoke in the morning, I would find myself thinking about the previous night's scripture, as well as other revelations and thoughts, and this would go on all day. More often than not, answers to questions or solutions I needed would manifest. I believe that the Spirit who knows all things can do that. He wants to do it more often but we need to prepare the ground of our spirit by cultivating it with the Word. Otherwise, we don't give him anything to work with. When Moses died, God told Joshua, "Be strong and very courageous...Keep this Book of the Law always on your lips; meditate on it day and night, so that you may be careful to do everything written in it. Then you will be prosperous and successful" (Joshua 1:7-8). The more of the Word you get into your spirit, the stronger you become in your mind. Now, the images that my mind sees are His words and His thoughts. I find myself responding to life rather than reacting.

Luke 18:2-8 (NIV) says:

> Then Jesus told his disciples a parable to show them that they should always pray and not give up. He said: "In a certain town there was a judge who neither feared God nor cared what people thought. And there was a widow in that town who kept coming to him with the plea, 'Grant me justice against my adversary.' For some time he refused. But finally he said to himself, 'Even though I don't fear God or care what people think, yet because this widow keeps bothering me, I will see that she gets justice, so that she won't eventually come and attack me!' And the Lord said, "Listen to what the unjust judge says. And will not God bring

about justice for his chosen ones, who cry out to him day and night? Will he keep putting them off? I tell you, he will see that they get justice, and quickly. However, when the Son of Man comes, will he find faith on the earth?"

This parable in Luke 18:2-8 (NIV) describes beautifully how we ought to pray—always. This woman desired justice from her adversary and wasn't going to stop coming to him until she got it. She was almost shameless in her plea for what she wanted. The unjust judge gave her what she wanted not because he was God fearing or because he cared about her; he just wanted her to go away and leave him alone. Thank goodness that we have a God who desires to give us all we need. All we have to do is believe that He is, and that He is a rewarder of those who diligently seek Him (Hebrews 11:6). My prayer life had to become like the widow because I had to learn to press in and not give up.

During the beginning of my journey, my prayers were just like the widow's pleas: I needed justice from my adversary the devil. I was fighting for my spiritual life. I was desperate to be free from the lies of my past and I needed God to rescue me. I had become like Jacob, when he said, "'I will not let you go unless you bless me'" (Genesis 32:26, NIV). As our prayer life becomes like this widow and our zeal for blessing becomes like Jacob, I believe it pleases the Lord because it causes us to lean closer into him and to trust him a little more. I believe it makes Him smile when we discover for ourselves that He truly is our answer for all things.

The Bible also says in Philippians 4:6 (NIV), "Do not be anxious about anything, but in every situation, by prayer and petition, with thanksgiving, present your requests to God." This scripture helped me save a lot of time in my life. Before I understood this verse, I would try to figure out things on my own. I would fret and worry a little bit, let days go by worrying a little, and then, as a last resort, I would come to God in prayer. I don't recommend this; it wastes a lot of time. Don't encourage the gray hairs to grow faster or the blood pressure to go higher than it needs to. Going to God first is the better way.

Later in my journey I learned the importance of praying the Word. The Bible says in Isaiah 55:11 (KJV), "So shall my word be that goeth forth out of my mouth: it shall not return unto me void, but it shall accomplish that which I please, and it shall prosper in the thing whereto I sent it." When you pray the Word, you pray a perfect prayer. When you pray the Word, you can be confident that you are praying His will. When you pray the Word, you can be assured your prayers will hit the target and be answered according to His will, which is what we desire anyway.

Words are seeds, and seeds over time turn into harvest. Galatians 6:7 (KJV) reminds us, "Be not deceived; God is not mocked: for whatsoever a man soweth, that shall he also reap." Don't believe the lie that the words you speak are not important. It's a serious thing. I challenge you to take inventory of your words for a day and listen to what comes out of your mouth. I did and I found my words tended to speak poverty, sickness and death. I would say things like "I can never afford that," "You make me sick," or "That scares me to death." I know it seems petty. It did to me at first too, until I started seeing the fruit of my words turn into poverty, sickness and death, whether it was a physical death or the death of a dream. As I continued to read God's Word, I learned that poverty, sickness and death are the curse of the law but the Word also says in Galatians 3:13 that Christ redeemed me from the curse of the law. I didn't have to speak that way anymore.

The key to having the right words is to make sure the right kind of seeds are going in. As my knowledge of the Word grew, I realized my eye and my ear gates were the window to my soul. Matthew 6:22 (NIV) says, "The eye is the lamp of the body. If your eyes are healthy, your whole body will be full of light."

Concerning your ears, you need to be careful with not only what you hear but also how you hear it. Mark 4:24 tells us how we hear a thing will determine the measure we receive. Paul prepares Timothy in 2 Timothy 4:4 (NASB) by warning him that if the church is not careful with what they hear, "they will turn their ears away from the truth and turn aside to myths."

Philippians 4:8 (NIV) says, "Finally, brothers and sisters, whatever is true, whatever is noble, whatever is right, whatever is pure, whatever is lovely, whatever is admirable—if anything is excellent or praiseworthy—think about such things." This really kept me focused on what the Lord would consider a good seed. I knew the kinds of seeds I was sowing by the fruit I reaped.

In Psalm 19:13-14 (NIV) David's prays:

> Keep your servant also from willful sins;
> may they not rule over me.
> Then I will be blameless,
> innocent of great transgression.
> May these words of my mouth and this meditation
> of my heart
> be pleasing in your sight,
> Lord, my Rock and my Redeemer.

I am a firm believer that the battle for the soul is in the mind. For about a year and a half, "no" was the word I uttered the most. Later, I was able to say, "It is written," but "no" was all I could get out at first. The wrong thoughts would come to me all day long. "No," I would respond. I would have images of lies play in my mind like a movie reel. Again, "No."

I lived 2 Corinthians 10:5 (KJV) until it became a part of me. It says, "Casting down imaginations, and every high thing that exalteth itself against the knowledge of God, and bringing into captivity every thought to the obedience of Christ." Anything contrary to the Word of God is ultimately trying to exalt itself above the name of Jesus. The Bible says there is no name higher. Philippians 2:9 (NIV) says, "Therefore God exalted him to the highest place and gave him the name that is above every name." If a thought, question, or image is trying to take the place of Jesus, cast it down and declare "It is written."

I want you to notice what happened to Jesus after the temptation in Luke 4. It says in Luke 4:14 (NIV), "Jesus returned to Galilee in the power of the Spirit, and news about him spread through the whole countryside." Every time you overcome temptation you return in power. You get stronger and stronger with every trial.

I will forever be chained to the truth because it is what set me free from the power of sin and death. I am on the path to righteousness, which has led me to the path of my destiny. My destiny is in God the Father, and this keeps me off the road of destruction which is a dead-end road called spiritual death (separation from Father God for eternity).

My exhortation to you is find the truth that is found only in the Word of God. Read it, meditate on it daily, and do what it says. It will ultimately save your life.

PART 3
THE FACE OF DECEPTION

CHAPTER I

DECEPTION

As I thought about this third section, I considered many different ways to teach about deception. I tossed around the idea of talking about the ins and outs of deception and revealing to you the who, what, when, where and why of the matter. I pondered the idea of looking at the many faces of deception and educating you on how to identify this culprit. Then I realized that many of the things I would talk about didn't help me from falling prey.

Instead, I want to use an illustration my pastor used from the pulpit. Have you ever wondered how bankers can spot counterfeit currency almost instantly? As a part of their training, they are taught what the real currency looks like, whether it's a $20 bill or a $100 bill. They are taught to recognize the symbols, the placement of those symbols, the grade of ink, the watermarks on the paper, the quality of paper itself, the seals and more. Rather than teaching their employees what the fake currency looks like, they teach them what the authentic currency looks like. In doing so, it makes the counterfeit easy to spot. During training, the employer repeatedly sees and touches the genuine, so when the false is presented, their mind computes that something is not right. It looks or feels different from the real they are used to seeing and touching.

In my life, I was taught what not to do, what not to say, and how not to look. I was taught a compilation of rules and procedures of what *not* to do with the false hope that if I just followed them everything would work out and I would stay out of trouble. Needless to say, if this had worked, there would be a different premise and title for this book. I will tell you the only fruit that came out of that upbringing (which included many years of my adult life) was bondage and a misunderstanding of who God really is. It was truth but without grace, and that turned into judgment resulting in a religious spirit.

I knew something wasn't right. I needed to figure out the pieces to life's puzzle. First, I needed to learn what the pieces looked like, and, second, I needed to understand how to arrange them so I would end up with a picture that represented who God really was.

CHAPTER II

GOD

In the beginning, Eve forgot two things: who she is and who God is. I also had to learn who I was, but first I had to learn who God is because I didn't have a clue. When Moses asked God what to tell the Israelites when he asks who sent him, God says, "'I AM WHO I AM. This is what you say to the Israelites: 'I AM has sent me to you'" (Exodus 3:14). May I suggest to you that God was not so concerned with Pharaoh knowing who He was as much as He with Moses knowing who He was. He was someone who had no beginning, no end. no lineage, no social identity, and no time or space restraints; He exists all by Himself. He is the only true God who was and is and always will be.

God is omnipresent which means He is everywhere at the same time. It means there is no place He cannot inhabit. He has no restrictions and no constraints, which means He is wherever you are.

In Psalm 139:7-12 (NIV), it says:

> Where can I go from your Spirit?
> Where can I flee from your presence?
> If I go up to the heavens, you are there;
> if I make my bed in the depths, you are there.
> If I rise on the wings of the dawn,
> if I settle on the far side of the sea,

even there your hand will guide me,
your right hand will hold me fast.
If I say, "Surely the darkness will hide me
and the light become night around me,"
even the darkness will not be dark to you;
the night will shine like the day
for darkness is as light to you.

We cannot exist anywhere God is not; you can't get away from Him. Have you ever tried desperately to get away from someone or something, yet they are there everywhere you turn? Psalm 139 says God is wherever we are. The Bible also says "he will never leave you nor forsake you" (Deuteronomy 31:6, NIV).

God is omniscient. He is all knowing. He knows the past, present and the future. Nothing takes Him by surprise. He knows everything and everything that will ever need to be known. Psalm 147:4-5 (KJV) says "He telleth the number of the stars; he calleth them all by their names. Great is our Lord, and of great power: his understanding is infinite." Psalm 44:21 says He knows the secrets of my heart. Proverbs 15:3 says his eyes are everywhere and He sees the good and the evil. Jeremiah 29:11 tells me He knows the plans for my life.

If you need to know something—an answer to a question, a solution to a problem, or wise decision that needs to be made—just ask Him. After you ask Him, sit, listen and wait to hear what He has to say. Unfortunately, many times I didn't receive it because I didn't ask. Please do not make my mistake.

1 John 5:14 (NLT) says, "And we are confident that he hears us whenever we ask for anything that pleases him." John 14:13-14 (NIV) reads, "And I will do whatever you ask in my name, so that the Father may be glorified in the Son. You may ask me for anything in my name, and I will do it." Whatever the question, Jesus is the answer. He is the all-knowing. You never have to live

with "I don't know" syndrome anymore, when you know the One who knows.

God is omnipotent. He is all powerful. There is nothing greater; there is nothing deeper or wider. His power has no limits! It is infinite. Psalm 113:5 (NIV) says "Who is like the LORD our God." Jeremiah 10:6 (ESV) says, "There is none like You, O LORD; you are great, and your name is great in might." In 1 Chronicles 17:20 (NKJV), it says, "O LORD, *there* is none like You, nor *is there any God* besides You, according to all that we have heard with our ears."

According to the Bible, God is light and there is no darkness in him (I John 1:5). He cannot lie (Titus 1:2). He is my strength and my refuge (Psalm 46:1), my rock and my salvation (Psalm 18:2) and my hiding place (Psalm 32:7).

Love is what drew me to Him. John 3:16 (NIV) says "For God so loved the world that he gave his only Son, that whoever believes in him shall not perish but have eternal life." Romans 5:8 tells me that while I was still a sinner Christ died for me. Romans 2:4 tells me that it was His goodness that led me to repentance.

CHAPTER III
IDENTITY

The essence of God is love, and, because I was made in His image, my core is also love. The truth is without Him I am nothing; with Him I am everything. If you have been told something else or if you believe anything different, it's a lie. You've been deceived. Know God, so you can know who you are and you won't easily fall into deception. God's thoughts are all that matters.

Identity is the key to your destiny, and this comes from the ultimate relationship with Father God. Knowing who you are and what rock you were cut from changes your outlook on life. This knowledge causes you to make different decisions, which leads you down different paths to different relationships.

When I was deceived, I moved away from my true identity. I had forgotten who I was. I had forgotten who God was. I started listening to what everyone else was saying about Him. I heard their doubts—how they weren't even sure He existed because, if He did, how could He let bad things happen? I began listening to all of their complacency and murmuring. They began filling my head with all of their ideology and what their interpretation of the truth was. These were people who I believed were sold out to the truth of the Word of God; I found out otherwise. These people had become their own god because they were choosing what was right and wrong in their own eyes. They had no boundaries and no point of reference to what was true.

I became like them because I listened to them. The reason why I can share this so pointedly is because this was also me—the face of deception. Not only did I begin to buy into all these misconceptions, but I began convincing others of the same mindset. I started blowing the same smoke out of the same pipe. I too had become my own god, deciding what was right from wrong.

I can only speak for myself but my twisted thinking came as a result of an offense that had turned to bitterness because of unforgiveness in my heart. I was mad at the world! I had become so toxic I began paving my own road to destruction.

If you relate, my advice to you is this: stop dead in your tracks, cry out to God like I did, find a copy of the Letter He wrote and begin reading it. Let your Father—the Creator, the God of the universe—begin to reveal Himself to you. As a result, you'll find out who you really are. Go ahead. He's waiting.

CHAPTER IV

Relationships

Once you have discovered your identity, then, and only then, can you escape this fiend called deception. No one can ever lie to you again about who God is or who you are. One thing I should tell you is that it's not enough to just know about God. He desires a relationship with you. He wants you to get to know Him. This is no different from getting to know a new friend. It requires spending time alone with Him and in community with those who are like-minded. We all must develop quiet time with God because He has secrets to tell you and mysteries that are only for you. In Jeremiah 33:3 (NASB), God says, "Call to Me and I will answer you, and I will tell you great and mighty things, which you do not know." In Ephesians 1:9 (NASB), it says, "He has made known to us the mystery of His will." In Jeremiah 29:11 (NIV), it says, "'For I know the plans I have for you,' declares the Lord, 'plans to prosper you and not harm you, plans to give you hope and a future."

Getting to know Him corporately is also important. I had to find a community. I am not designed to be alone. In the beginning, God knew that it was not good for Adam to be alone (Genesis 2:18). After naming all the animals, there was "no suitable helper found" (Genesis 2:20, NIV). He needed the fellowship of another human. Fellowship is a key to growth and success, not only in your walk with God, but for life's successes in general. Proverbs

11:14 (KJV) says, "Where no counsel is, the people fall: but in the multitude of counselors there is safety."

My daughter often led small groups in our home. They often study through a dvd or a book series. I love their discussion times! Someone would ask a question or a statement might be made and then they'd talk about it. The insights were so rich. Each one had his/her own idea or revelation, and it was so amazing to listen to. Each comment built upon another and another. It was not one person with all the answers. Many times one person would have one part and another person would give the missing element. When it was all brought together, what an exhibit of inspiration it was! It was like a whirlwind of synergy that exploded in the room.

I believe this is a picture of what a community in relationship with Jesus is supposed to look like. Hebrews 10:24-25 (NIV) says, "And let us consider how we may spur one another on toward love and good deeds, not giving up meeting together, as some are in the habit of doing, but encouraging one another—and all the more as you see the Day approaching." I think we can all agree that the days we live in are treacherous and deceitful; being alone can be kind of intimidating. This could be why the Lord is in favor of togetherness.

CHAPTER V

ABSOLUTELY

Don't allow culture to drive you. God never changes nor does His words. We should never allow our circumstances or what's going on around us to get into us, especially if it is counter to the truth of God. Don't be shake; instead be settled and confident in the One you believe in. Seasons will come and seasons will go, but He remains. He is the same God in the winter as He is in the summer. He is the same God on the mountain as He is in the valley.

I allowed cancel culture to get inside me. When the Word of God (or truth) didn't line up with what was going on in my world, then I just canceled it and replaced it with what I wanted the truth to be. My friends didn't stop me because they were doing the same thing. As a result, I became blind and foolish in the way I thought about the way of the world. I began to get lost in ideologies and beliefs that I knew were wrong; I didn't care at the time because of my own brokenness. I forgot my own identity. I didn't know who I was anymore and I certainly didn't know who God was.

I was told for a lot of my adult life that there was no such thing as absolutes. I was told they just didn't exist. I would see signs that said something was free. Yet, my dad would say nothing in this world is free; he would say somebody somewhere is paying for it. It wasn't absolutely free. Have you ever been in conversation with someone and heard them answer "Absolutely?" Or maybe you've seen an advertisement for a new ride at a local theme park and upon investigating the ride and contemplating whether you would ride it or not, you've answered "Absolutely not."

I learned that without absolutes in my life, I was destined to be deceived. As the adage goes, "If you don't stand for something, you will fall for anything." I had to decide to never be a victim of deception again. I made up my mind to have my answer before the question is even raised. I settled within my heart what the truth of the Word of God said and when a question would arise (because it will), I already knew how to respond. Truth is truth. It doesn't become less truth because your culture changed. The Bible says "Jesus Christ is the same yesterday and today and forever" (Hebrews 13:8, NIV). God is absolute perfection. God is absolute light. He is absolute love. He is also the absolute judge. I had to settle within myself that there is someone way bigger than me.

Deception and mixture go hand in hand. The reason why deception is so successful is because there is usually some truth in deception, just enough to cause you to question. This is the same device the enemy used on Eve in the garden from the beginning. A foolish person will only see the truth and look past the lie because it allows them to be enticed by their own appetite for sin. This was me. If I could find any justification to indulge, then I did.

CHAPTER VI
MY HOPE

My downfall began here: I forgot my identity and I didn't know my God. As a result of these two follies, I became my own god. This took me down a road full of more than I bargained for. Sin will always take you further than you want to go and take more than you want to give.

Deuteronomy 30:19 (NKJV) says, "I call heaven and earth as witnesses today against you, *that* I have set before you life and death, blessing and cursing; therefore choose life, that both you and your descendants may live." God gives you the choice, then He tells you which one to choose. My hope is that you choose life.

Printed in the United States
by Baker & Taylor Publisher Services